TILT

Hartill   Hool   Jones

TILT

The Collective Press

The Collective Press
Penlanlas Farm
Llantilio Pertholey
Y-Fenni
Gwent
NP77HN

Cover design

Cataloguing In Publication Data for this book is available from the British Library.

ISBN 1 899449 30 2

The publisher acknowledges the financial assistance of the Welsh Arts Council.

'Celtic Bird' by Christina Scurr.

Back cover photograph by Phil Martin.

Printed by Redwood Books, Trowbridge.

Typeset in Goudy by

For
Daniel;
Mikka & Kiki;
Aneirin & Rebecca.

Contents

Graham Hartill
From the Dragon's Head: 12 Black Mountain poems

Ric Hool
Looking down like looking up

John Jones
For reasons other than strength

Foreword

These poems are assembled to great all-round benefit. Unrhymed, rhythmic patterns in which metre is subtly observed when observed at all, in which metre is often suspended altogether leaving the syllables to take their own rhythmic shapes from page space, dense obtuse lining and natural breath, it would be easy, at first glance, to ascribe to them all the compositional techniques developed at Black Mountain, North Carolina. To assume such blanket similarity is misleading. The work is radically varied, each poet finding vastly different resonance's in the landscape of South Powys and Gwent.

Graham Hartill's work takes its place naturally in the tradition of those poets with roots in the work of Ezra Pound and T.S. Eliot who enjoy landscape by envisaging scenarios from its history. Hartill, like Basil Bunting, David Jones, Alan Fisher or Tom Meyer, often adopts the personae of historical figures through whom to speak, a geomancer, a Roman soldier, the Kilpeck shielaghnagig. Architectural details hold the poet in a constant thrall of identification. Through this excitement he captures the ongoing breathless beauty of the weather and the light. Literary space, the simplicity and elegance of his words in their groups, echoes the very spaces and washes of light that enhance his explorations perpetually. This is the virtuoso work of a sophisticated craftsman who, despite his mature professionalism, retains a simple religious quality.

The other two poets are not so fortunate nor so supported by tradition. They are uneasy isolated souls carving short epistles of solace out of experiences which are more a dilemma than an exploration.

John Jones looks at the self-same hills that fill Hartill
with such delicate flights of astonishment. He is a farmer and he
encounters the land at unselected times. For him the landscape
that is Hartill's treasure scape, pleasure trigger and holy land, is
an implacable, indifferent, indeed often hostile place of work.
"A farm" he says he "thinks to own" but which he finds "owns
him." Enactments of death, images of death, actual deaths of
stock and vegetation are frequent in the work as though the life
of the land were unimportant when taking place in such crass
silence. The verse, then, the opposite of lyrical. The spaces are
important whether the reader sees them as blank paper or silent
time, emphasising honed and polished groups of words that
separate them. The words themselves are terse and taciturn,
taking the monosyllables and the stoicism of the countryman and
enhancing it, so that it becomes poetic rhetoric, sledgehammer
blows of economy and understatement dealt by a powerful man
who finds himself helpless.

Ric Hool lives on the other side of Llanelly Hill. If there
are ghosts of the past there, they are more recent industrial
ghosts. The land is a vast wreckage space remaining from the
days of its productiveness. Lined along the hillsides are the
housing estates, cracked memorials to a lost Socialist optimism,
grim terraces, rabbit warrens where industrial workers formed
their own support systems as they always do, where their
grandchildren remain, weirdly stranded between the colour video
and the new kitchen unit, edging their way around one another,
wary with boredom. Hool then is a poet of the domestic situation
and the domestic interior. His verse forms inch their way through
careful, considered lines that have a sense of being deliberately
half-completed as though the poet wanted the sentences to leak
into each other.

cont . . .

There is nothing bizarre in the people who inhabit the house of Hool. The difficulties are everybody's problems of flawed communication, generational discord, aborted dreams and ambitions. The work has a fragile bitterness, a wry weariness that finds a certain grace in the tensions between individuals who, as individuals always do, fall short of one another's expectations but still cannot find it in themselves to let one another down.

The differences here, rural ancient , rural contemporary, urban post-industrial, highly trained, self taught, virtuoso expertise, wilful technical idiosyncrasy, happily and properly illustrate the policy of individual variety the Abergavenny Collective pursues.

It is also apposite that all three poets write about Monmouthshire (Gwent) which has never really known if it was wholly Welsh or half English. It is clear, with such subject matter, that work doesn't have to be Welsh to be good, nor English to be bad. The criticism we apply is literary, not political, not tribal, and not racist.

Jeff Nuttall 1996

Graham
Hartill

From the Dragon's Head:
12 Black Mountain poems

TILT

Graham Hartill

Has lived in Wales on and off since the early seventies and in the Black Mountains since 1992. His publications include collaborative translations of Chinese poetry, the influences of which can be felt in much of the work included here.

From the Dragon's Head is the writer's homage to the remains of a past which continues to discharge soul into the present.

Bronzes (Milvus-Milvus 1988); Turas (Red Sharks 1988); The Songs Of My Heart (translations, 1988) and Ruan Ji's Island /(Tu Fu) In The Cities (1992, both Wellsweep).

First Moon: at the Dragon's Head

......*ssiang!*

daylight

stroking the silver strings

*

listen -

mist -

sifting the stones and reflective laurel

the house a heron

rising out of the black pool

*

ssiang!......

I wake again from a dream of ruins

      this house is a book -

         chimney

         window

         roof

         scalp

         & eye

         & tooth

*

somedays we see the herons along the river -
where do they sleep I wonder?

and how the ancestors?

*

if they're not planted fast, it's said

their hair will grow for ever

somewhere the heron lifts like light

from the black river

*

                    path

                    & wall

                    & crocus shoot

                    vein

                    & rib

                    & foot

a shovel clangs on far-off tar

a sparrow singing

  "here
   I was born"

*

the Winter dawn

stroking her silver strings

     *

Note to First Moon:

"The songs contain a number of meaningless cries or exclamations and
at the caesura of each line is the exclamation *hsi* which may represent
the panting of the shaman in trance. One might expect the Spirit to
speak through the the shaman's mouth. The shaman, says a writer of
the first century A.D., strikes the dark strings (probably a shaman name
for a kind of zithern) and brings down the dead who speak through his
mouth."
-Arthur Waley in his introduction to The Nine Songs: A Study of
Shamanism in Ancient China.

"The Dragon's Head" is my local pub, in the village of Llangenny at the
foot of Sugar Loaf, in the Black Mountains.

Sky Burial - Skirrid Fawr

At the end of the Shining Path, along the ridgeback, there is a sharper rise to the peak. The falling fields were misty, the ridge itself was yellow in the light, and a pair of crows were perched ahead of us as black and as big as vultures.

They took off. The last time we came here there was a ring of ashes round the pinnacle - by then it had mostly filtered into the turf. Today we saw the shuddering blue of a tilted beetle clambering over the grasses, and a thick red lazy erecting bull.

It feels like a place for an Autumn Sky Burial, meaning a wide sculpture of time and material - the blonde grains of a grasscrop arranged in a diamond, a breast or mouth being stuffed with feathers, a peak made of parchment to draw a circle.

*

Woodpecker, if you are anywhere near, nail me a house, and everybody bring up stones, as if to a cairn, to hold its shape against the loss of memory, the brain's dissolving.

The fields spread out to the bluff and the tube revolves, patterns of grass and cloud falling again to a different colour.

*

The Geomancer

I know the lie of the land,
  its bone and blood
the back of my hand,
the run
  of the black and the white water.

Here's my gourd,
my blanket
and my man of straw
to shield you from the living face
  of the demon dead -
I stand my ground at the Dragon's Head.

Listen -
  I exhale the buried cities -
"Cambalu and Samarkand by Oxus,
Paquin, Negus and Melind"
and Battersea, in rainy winter evening's green and yellow lights.
  I strike the strings.

My song is just a territory
being shaped, becoming known.
My chant accelerates like water
falling black and white
  through streambed stones.

I know the lie of the land,
my head and hands
  your mountain and your wood.
Their steps,
    their doorways opening and shutting
in your heart,
  let drift your bone and blood.

          *

St. Martin's Church, Cwmyoy.
(for the New Year, 1994)

The earth is rucked by thousands of years of landslip -
   the "Cwm of the Yoke" - and ridden with mud after weeks
                                                    of rain.

   St. Martin's Church is riven, but bucks at every side
the quick and the slow storms
   of weather, expression, geology -

this is the kick of recurring discovery:
   twisting words or wrenching clay
      to mould some truth from the groundswell -

   one by one, we climb the quivering ladder to shadows
                                          and bells.

                        *

To a Winged Head
(at Patricio Church)

ask a lot
of the slippery paths
& the red-wet leaves,
the day
& you
to speak to me -

the church is very cold
& now the sky is hurtling past the hill
with slashing sails of hail and light
   if this is what it takes
it takes all day
to get from where your face is recognised
to red, the blue and yellow
that soften the sky over Cennau's slope

   the Water-Dragon snarls & slaps his tail
the length of the Grwyne
leave it now
& let the night accumulate
leaves & rain
the length of the lane
to my very door

                    *

Jesse
(the monumental remains of a carving in the Priory
Church of St. Mary, Abergavenny)

From high in his gut -
          it is blackened by wars
              and polished by secret
      sweat of hands as many as mountain-days,
                  as dark as Pentwynglas
                  under cloud-crawl -

Jesse
         pushes the oak-shaft
               up from the wine and the pulp
         still in him -

         this he births

      to shoot through the architecture,
          history's vanishing point,
              trailing ancestor-leaves
              and lifting,
                  lifting a crown
                      where Somebody sits
              like a purple and yellow flower.

                  *

The rings of his sleep
              are as hard as oak,
        his cloak and his ankles are oak,
              his beard is curly
                    and hard as clouds and rock,
              his eyes are oak -

        I stand in the darkening nave,
            November,
          watching Jesse's future-flower
              buckle and drift
                    like a Neon Tetra
        deep in the heads of his tribe,
            we free and foresaken millions.

                    *

An Exile's Letter

These are my rooves and bridges
    these my tracks in mud -
  this is my radio
      mopping the people's rage,
I turn the river's page

      (which is, after all, as good as mine -
       for every day I drag my fuel from its edges)

  the mountain's ditches

and silver stones

  are daily,

     syllable by syllable,

    becoming known -

I learn their forms,
   their forms of patience,

     working alone.

    *

The Invaders

Defeat: A Javelin
(from a Northern river, the memory-frontier of a Roman soldier slain in battle)

But listen, I have forgotten -
   my life is a skyful of moonlight covered with cloud,
  a yellow ghost
     patrols the midnight limit.

I speak, but I have forgotten -
   my brain is a hillful of trees, their roots ripped up
     by a wind that slammed into my helmet
               with your javelin.

      *

So, I lost my head -
   it floated down the channel
keenly observed by the Kingfisher.

No, it's better not to wear this necklace of shimmering roads,
   this head-dress of hills
and the signs that swerve in the midnight sky

when they all insist on a time like this -
   our teeth like fallen bridges,
our voices the tremble of owls.

      *

The shields and the poles of our enemies clogged and stirred
                                                    the stream -
    our army died on television,
buzzing, in a pool of dots,
            the papers full of photographs of peasants
        stripping down the implements and emblems of our law -

No, it's better not to know the language any more -
    we came to bring a mountain's law to the hills
        and highways to the pitted tracks.

            Now the moon is rattling in its socket,
                our speeches bleach and dissolve
                    against the bluff.

            *

We got this far.

        The rivers of the North roll on
            to the unattainable coast.

        *

Victory: A Dance On The Llywel Stone

        our prow pushes open
        the Summer river -
          starlings and lanterns

           *

        push between fields which ripple and
                 comb -
          Maccutrenus! -
            we've snapped off the head of your
                 one black rock
            and stuck it the other way up

           *

        with insect eyes patrolling the purple
                 hedges,
         (Summer holly)
          speaking in ripples and kites,
           a zigzag of sweatmen and stickmen
               and cattle,
             ours -
          cracked between cwms and garns

           *

our speeches rage and dissolve
   over Mynydd Troed
where I was manned,
   shaking my javelin pearls from its tip

                    *

worldwork -
   one by one
the stonesweight
   in the pasture wall

   your curses fuel it

                    *

31

At Kilpeck Church

These Herefordshire carvers hacked into stone
         as if it were daylight,

freeing such as a 'bear', that devours 'children',
a 'bird' that regurgitates something
into a 'human' mouth,

an angel, falling from Spacetime,
knot of stone.

These men of Herefordshire knew what they were doing,
           chewing stone as if it were night and day.
The rain behaves like love or leprosy,
pouring from lips yanked wide
in grins or is it grimaces?
splashing centuries of
craving,
laughing,
swearing by day and night.

This Friday afternoon the two of us standing here,
straining for detail,
knotting the branches of torment and insight.

      *

(for Richard Lanham)

32

The New Year

The year began like a damp fox
stretching its paw from the hedge.
We slept till late, and when we rose
the valley to the south was full of mist,
the sky above the mountains yellow in the rain.
Sparrows scratched on the tin of the caravan roof,
the trees stood cold and empty, rising
from their hoops.

Walking the River Wye
our minds, beside each other,
drifted - when we spoke it tended to be of
the same thing at the same time.
This was a time when wealth
was gathered to the businessmen, the gamblers -
                    Tao Yuan Ming
lay scorn on every aspect of government business,
tending his path and his pasture, rewarding his friends
                    for their help
with a bottle of wine.

The river was full to its banks and grey
with the strength of an army.
South, in Gloucestershire, the trains were blocked
and could not pass.
                    He wrote:
'The empty boat glides on -
whoever comes must go -
the ups and downs can never touch our freedom"
emptying his jug of Kiangsi wine.

And drinking wine all night
they poured themselves over the ancient poems
sorting out all the differences of interpretation.

The river was constantly glancing
through the gulleys and the hedges,
regarding us, retreating
under the iron sky, that twisted,
turning like an ancient poem.

*

(for Ursula)

Knotwork

1
(The font at Eardisley)

The   Rescue:

Slanting towards the left, away from the lion,
(good or bad, with his good and his bad
eye)
is it Jesus
pulling the man away?
    He is sloping, flying,
Jesus clutching his wrist
and around his feet are the lacing knots

which is the *Book*

that pulls to further, never-ending knotting,
timeless binding of cause-and-effect.

It is branches,
            branches and serpents,
armour,
            and leaves that are also armour.

Is it a saint
that clutches this book to his breast?

The Soldier

and the knots go on.
The soldier hides
in branches, yet he is bound in them,
convulsed in them, since Eden.

Every day
his spear ruptures the enemy's thigh,
they are plaited in fighting
and this wound,
                    or this killing,
could be where the carver started, or

the Lion

following them.
                    The wound leads on to the lion,
the font is a chasing, a bowl
of roads and sinews
looping through Saxony,
Angle-land's eastern fields,
the North and West.

I am, the carver says, a Viking and a Celt,
a writhing catholic from Spain
through Parthenay-le-Vieux perhaps
to here, Herefordshire.

Nobody knows my name.

I am the carved,
    my sinew-strings, my heart-knots
will finish as Shobden's soft pink arches -
weathered, no longer readable things.

2
(Kilpeck)

There is no way out of the eating,
Kilpeck's virgin/whore is all devouring,
all disgorging

- "this is my body."

She says let loose your monkey-mind
and let it dance
from knot to knot:

where fish eats man
eats bear
is fish

eats bird
is foliate head
is falling man

who plunges to ecstasy,
plunges to ego,
to eating,

to Image

- "this is my sex, my visage."

Only my ritual work, the carving says,
            resolves the process:
Kilpeck's beakheads, smiling, birthing

- take and eat. This is it, my body.

Get up close and trace the knot with your fingertip,
            your dogeared notebook, close-up lens,
and stroke the joys and the sufferings

- this is my double sex, of eye and chisel
something of the god you bring.

3
(Temple Guardians, Kunming, South China)

We howl slaughter
we tread lions
stretching our mouths to ferocious deltas.

Earlobes wrenched to shoulders,
eyes globes being sucked from orbit,
ribs waves, thrashing on mountains,
waves of mountains.

Darts and charges twist in our fingers
banners fume about our necks.
     On the stiff wind
            of our will and volition
we brandish hoops of forgotten purpose,
serpents, dragons, fiends and tiny spheres for unknown reasons -

no-one can pass us by -
there is no getting past the mirrors that catch the sun in our
chest and foreheads,
no getting past your face.

*

And when its done the poem
leans or lies like a carved ball -
curlicues and drifts of stone
and oak-leaves wreathing a smiling face,
propped on a pillar, or flat on the winter floor
of Abbey Dore.

Ric
Hool

Looking down like looking up

TILT

Ric Hool

Has lived as an 'outsider' in Hastings and Spain since leaving Newcastle in 1979. He repeats this experience in Wales where he has lived since 1990. He is witness to a world in transition; of images in fast black lines.

Looking down like looking up. The perspective and orientation of this writer's vision are elements of his writing process.

Fitting in with Malcolm (Wysiwyg Chapbooks 1993); Heterosexual Honkies (Wysiwyg Chapbooks 1994).

Mums and Dads

They watch our emotions unwrap:
taste the syrup; the acidity

clenched in teenage hormones;
can't see themselves settle

in a love of leftovers
like an out of season resort.

Doing their own thing, then
coming together as clashed cymbals

bringing overture to overture
around mealtimes.

In spite of mums and dads
we end up (mostly) as

mums and dads
concocting new flavours -

passion removed to something
like Benidorm in January.

Kitchen

Peanut butter
sandwich with whisky,
her conversation and
a white wall
viewed through the window.

An archipelago of thoughts
erupt; collapse; leave
atoll-shaped memories.

Looking down,
a predictable symmetry of tiles
fall tidily underfoot
- clean as a good marriage -
I lean against
the lip of the sink.

As hard as people try,
kitchens will not be
disordered places.

Tins for things are uniform,
a shelf of jars;
surfaces made for wiping.

Something heavy crashes.
I recognise the shards
as fragments of decision.
Do you wonder how
an atoll is reefed?

How a wild notion
is pricked
by the pin
of a single second?

While you consider

a pan and brush appear.

End of Century Family

Rolls, Kerouacs of paper
stammered with words - can
thoughts survive this?

A movement in the corner
of my eye, you, busy,
nail on skin, a spot
to be covered by tomorrow's make-up.

You say something.
It pinballs, da-da-da,

between the end and
beginning of two ideas
tapped on manuscript.

You manipulate
my under-thought reply
joint to socket.

The living room is amphitheatre
around a small window on life:
a front row of interactive kids
blissed on information highway.

Outside, Mynydd James
is in its two hundred
and thirteenth,
millionth year.

Here we are,
shuffling around
in silly-character bedroom slippers,
excruciatingly caring.

Man at Ladies' Hairdresser

It is where pared curls are swept:
a mojo-hand to trance a lover.

A theatre of acts play.

First and second fingers,
reminiscent of a wrestler's legs,
force hair into submission;

blades snip
in fast conversation.

Regimental curlers troop colours
on skin-pinched skulls
to a backdrop of radio-pop
and B^b driers.

Lotions; sprays racked; assertive
looks and words ping...
all done by mirrors.

Echo Sounding

I touch her hair and know
there have been small changes
since we finger-curled and
love-locked ourselves in rings.

The whiteness, lacing, icing
of connubial ideals
float vaporously over
a lumping, deep ocean.

Kids exploded our oneness;
unmeshed nets and knots
tightly tied
without grasp
of other forces.

Love played Ping-Pong between us -
no complication. Now
it echoes like sonar:
mother/daughter,
father/wife,
husband/daughter.

Bombing

The bomber
loosed a whistle,

a roar bloomed:
kick-off at Wembley.

Looking down like looking up
on Guy Fawkes' Night.

Later - and problems lighter -
the bomber landed.

Someone had stacked more worries
next to the runway . . .

real as a nightmare.

51

A Canvas on South Wales

Watchet, looking north;
the night clear enough
though low cloud hammers
reflected blue-purple-pink light
back to the sparked, brash coast
                    on South Wales.

Extraterrestrial but
that's what being alone
in an empty, dark place
                    brings on
                        &
lyrics of a tune you never knew you knew.

From this range, at this time,
it is almost Fauvist,
awaiting a Dufy
to put some fast black lines
over the backfield of colour
to make it work.

As if it were that easy -
and on a cold night, wrapped warm, everything is -
that poisonous prism
hanging over there
would be a rainbow.

I saw potato eaters on TV

Throwback faces
jowled
mouths ready to bite
huddle darkly around a knife of light.

Potatoes bond tomorrow
with today's resolution.

The almost show-nothing of night

captured

they hear shells burst
before they are fired.

after *Potato Eaters* by Vincent Van Gogh

The Kiss

Arrived
returned
this place

my tiger
your tongue

inside.

Hummingbird
Hoovered-up
breath.

Lips unseal;
all fractured
by the first
spoken word.

(Door of Paradise: Gate of Hell.)

Painting by Numbers

for Jackson Pollock

Coagulated red held good
        then haemorrhaged into a delta.

Beatific highways of language hitched
           to unfixed destinations

upward and across
        the continent of cloth.

The drip: alcohol, petrol, blood.

Sayonara Bet

for Coronation Street

That cat,
those rooftop-trumpet notes
dreary as slates
predictably slanted

                rain
on hunched shoulders.

Heal-worn relationships
                revisited
over dialect-thrummed
conversation.

A maraschino death.
The blonde
walks out!

Lights dip,
measured
in half-a-million
boiled electric kettles...

click.

A Poor Response to an SOS

llfracombe beach   where
because he sat there long enough   dreams
wrecked on bladed rocks   were stolen
pecked by gulls

                                        shovelled
                                        turned
                                        patted-out.

His fingers selected parts
skimmed them: dot-dot-dot
dash-dash-dash
dot-dot-dot
across waves.

Not a lifeguard in sight
only this stranger
whose consoling palm
- too scared to be incriminated -
turned a coin over
in his pocket.

Stretching a Point

Infinity is in the imagination.

What appears to be
an infinitely long line
could be

a huge circle,

which might be
the forearm of a gigantic 4

or
the crossing of an enormous T.

That parenthesis
that dashed us apart
optimistically
could be
the smallest fraction of a loop

that will rejoin us.

Take-off

I see but still can't believe;
know it is crucial
air flow is slower
above than below
the cut of wings.
Thrust too, must
defeat drag.

There it is above me now
dripping an Action Painting;
glinting a winning grin
to my doubting eye.

My medieval mind cowers
to feet
which start to run.

Arms out, curved back,
faster
till my lungs aren't there;
fingers tight and tilted
in a wish.

Inside a Wild Night

Gales wail,
things crunched,
the night
eaten slow-
ly.

Get up;
listen to nature
being unnatural-
ly disturbing,
lifting the skin
off a garage;

taking the scalp from a house;

tearing the space between fences.

The stillness inside
is the ear of the storm
and I, smaller,
more insecure
than silence.

In Confidence

(No don't
say a word,
not one
or she'll know.

Not one
single word, not
a single syllable
or she'll know.

Know it was me
in my northern slang
kicking cans of words
down dirty gutters
along doorstepscrubbedstreets.

Repeat.
Don't say a word,

not one.)

Thoughts on Driving Nos. 1 & 2

1. By night,
when you drive as much,
distance is an enemy.

A clear road is a liquorice
you roll up
complete with a pink sweet
at the centre.

Daytime - and there are too many
sweets and too little liquorice -
distance is still an enemy
so close between bumpers.

2. Night and day
are tonal opposites
in which attempts are made
to avoid so much
in camouflage.

War Children

The field screams to disorder
belly-up with boils;
soil-rained lumps
patter the ground.

One thousand demands
blister tree bark,
newsprint takes them further.

The field consumes
the toil of peace;
the work of war,

immediately ready
for children to explore
new dens and start
healing games.

Rain in Los Boliches

In Los Boliches
whenever it rains
we go out,
stand,
look up and melt like candles.

Rifle shots of water
ricochet off
the armour of the street;
squalls machine gun
up and down
                    then stop.

Closed windows sob;
bubbles breathe from pavements.

Returning indoors
our clothes cover less.
We see each other differently
cotton become
a transparent skin.

Working in Northern Spain

Day crackles on the car radio.
We talk over it and touch.

The road breaks into Alcover
past its monstrous church
moving up, out of town
to my place.

Dust and rock,
a cloth of almonds grow
here and there...

time is a jacket
put in; taken out of a wardrobe.

John
Jones

For reasons other than strength

TILT

John Jones

Lives and works as a stockman in the Black Mountains. They are his ancestoral and spiritual home, as such they are the major source of inspiration for his poetry. In a landscape rich and vibrant, chambered with a chaotic past, he strikes a living from its present realities. Here he takes a harsh world head-on.

For reasons other than strength continues the struggle to confront and define some god's universe.

Tug (Anvil 1991);
Heterosexual Honkies (Wysiwyg Chapbooks 1994);
Blind Cwm (The Collective 1992) and Lucifer's
Cradle\1993.

Being God

I am god
not the whole god
but part of it

if I spill my blood
and the blood could speak
it would say

I am the man
not the whole man
but part of it

when I lift the soil
it says
I am the earth

and I listen
and offer no argument

when I kill
and eat the flesh
there is only silence.

Lying Here   .
loci of a point

                    I

               watch

          for reasons

     other than strength

amid this green grass

     growing   design

          amongst unseated

               stones that from their

                    lodge lie blindly

                         sentinels to other rocks

                              in all this fucking space.

The Golden Flying
Half Stunned Thing

lying on its back
trod air
convulsed
by the reading lamp
it failed to read
till late

rapt into the light
fallen
twisting
like words
a being half watched
closed   to the edge.

Farther Father

My son plays
        amongst the fallen
       trees   become jungle

  become tiger

  become memory

  become barefoot
  in shadow

  shaded
             till the hunted
  knowing the game

     rolls back its eyes
       and plays dead.

Being Polite

The photo is a dead man
   becoming
      a photograph of me

         a memento
         at least.

               Framed in silver
                  it talks
                     beguiling conversation

                     then static
                        leaning back
                           we gather dust.

Particles

Nose bleeds and throat
raw from breathing dust

            dry red dust
            I own and farm

or think to own
and in the thinking
find it owning me.

              These are not words

I care to breath loudly
      more whispers

                  like the red dust
                half whistling its way
            to my lungs in deep sleep.

they are wasted
like my Uncle

            from breathing
                deeper ground.

Culture I assume

              is a question of colour

and depth?

        old workings that are still

          raw can be fresh

This is my experience
            my experience
        and my Uncle's lungs

are family.

Excavators

The wagtail
the diesel
and me

scalping soil
with a silver
bucket

our yellow arm
picking through
its many colours

finding ground
stuffed with stones

a past experience

the wagtail
the diesel
and me

turning things over.

The Working Glove

Glove reflects
straining wire
more than that
the strain on limbs
that function in a place
        of sweat and grime.

The barrier   removed
another glove revealed
in living flesh a blown
benefactor of dead skin
stitched so I can finger you
and not be thought uncouth.

Hands In Winter

Skin catches first
an annoyance
each catch
a slight tear
each cold day

further separation

flesh splits

into the quick

and the dead.

Parliament for Wales

Blodau'r Pen

This May we died
like frosted flowers

an act of passing
outweighed by
a lack of past

stillborn
to an age of darkness

A Fine Thing

It rains a lot in Wales
and when it does
we speak of it.

We say a lot in Wales
except when it rains
then we gag while it passes.

Blind Cwm

When the bark splits
        shafted by winter
and the hollows freeze
    when the sloe berries
        bleed fire into gin
    and the melt of leaves
            become crack
    when the dogs are ice
        and the sheep
    stock-still in snow
        or under it
    when the sun
blisters nothing
    who cares.

Shark Fin Soup

Eating you
I consume
the terror
in being
fare

•

Small Game

White crows rising
from naked bones
into the narrow
Autumnal sky
circle like leaves
around the roosting tree
until the sound
of someone clapping
is reassessed
an insubstantial thing.

to Frank Olding

Chwarae Bach

Brain gwyn
a gwyd
o noethni esgyrn
i nefoedd cul
cynhaeaf,
a gylcha fel y dail
ynghylch y goeden glwyd
nes adasesu
sŵn y curo dwylo'n
ddim o beth.

Sanctuary

We shelter here
beneath the lungs of trees
where small birds jive
and dive to dryer pockets.

Colours of the males
dissolve in lights
divide by branch
through the lens cap canopy of leaves.

Water marks this envelope
droplets of sound rebound
and pass this glade
to invade
and redefine their print on open land.

Small wonder
that the bees cease fire mid hum
until the flattened hay
creaks quiet
resurrected in the resurrected sun.

A Pot Shot @
Pol Pot's Parrot

The dead bird
bird shot
beak down
pointing down
the down slope
of the concrete
yard
looked disappointed

●

To be shot
in the four slot
this morning
by a man
in slippers
unmistakably
opposed
to its music.

Stone Stable
Midnight

Outside this darkness
distant suns blink time
through missing slates.

Here I watch
my stallion's eyes
that from the dark
watch mine like suns

the space between us
ever more important
than the space apart.

Shed

The roof's patter
    has a flat sound
        without felt

            somehow
           without feeling

    no fabric
    beneath slate
      but the bones
      of dowelled timber

          nothing to bounce
              sound against
          but perforations of worm

wood declines

and the stone
        ground

sticks like flesh
to the spine of the hill

        listen

          the hill
        has a flat sound

    somehow . . .without feeling . . .

Retro-gradient

The flailing head
      hangs the hedge
          passes on the line
   tractors into distance
then disappears

the engine farmers
diesel note dying
in the bright Autumnal fog.

Vapoured
like time into distance
it left the bones behind
with me
         suspended

   above an unobscured road.

Lucifer's Cradle

The same sky clouds
as it clears you
droplets pattern my cheeks
as the sun strokes yours

winter

you say that time
is the healer
but time like a leper
bears its own disease.

Jerusalem Lane

This track is a wheel rut
worn wide by passing time
this shambolic tree its edge
whose thorns dart nothing
but the dancing darkness
of biting midge

the only thing with teeth these days

compacting grains
masticulating time into tarmac
roughing up the feet
of passers by
who treat their blisters
like a penance paid

as if they resurrect the pilgrim
from amidst the tourist trade.

No Style

The stock fence
taught   against
the broken banks
of tumbled stone
and   layered   turf

        walls the sheep
        from tar strips
        that race   a-
        round the flesh
        of green fields

and either keeps
       the cretins in
or keeps the cretins out.

Blood House   (Ty Coch)

Strangers   passing
        built this place
    drove iron stays to walnut
                before leaving
shot pheasants
hang there
spotting blood on the flagstone floor.

Someone   then
found wood enough
to feed the fires crimson
cured ham and lava bread
cockles
on the outer rims black heat.

Someone gathered sloes to gin
married them in pickle jars
and let them bleed
        times stains into purple.

Devouring all this by the fat light
we stitch our patterns to a shawl
        in a closed corner
we carry our living to sleep
in the dust of our skin.

Outside
someone else
feeds the emptiness of stars
to a hollow sky.

In The Hedgerow, Something . . .

There is a different sound
between the languid bee
held within a haze
of nectar
                    and the quick probing
                      of fat flies   snared
                        within the scent
                          of rotting meat

        seems that flowers
aren't as fast as flesh
even in decay.

Notes on Poems

The Golden Flying Half Stunned Thing   71
   A self portrait.

Particles   74
   (Original title 'Drought is not a Welsh word')
   Draws on concepts of alienation, the original title refering to
   the root construction and meaning of both words.

Small Game   82
   The term 'White Crows' has been used by first language Welsh
   speakers to describe their countrymen who, with English as
   their first language, learn Welsh and compete at Eisteddfodau.
   Neither 'Small Game' or its accompanying translation would be
   eligible for consideration at these pinnacles of Welshness. With
   thanks to Frank Olding whose help in its translation 'Chwarae
   Bach' was considerable.

A Pot Shot @ Pol Pot's Parrot   84
   To 'artists' who, ducking their own countries harsh regimes,
   take the freedom of expression won in ours for granted.

Retro-gradient   87
   An old road rises at one end of this man's farm, it takes its
   name from Judge Jeffries 'The Hanging Judge' who travelled its
   length in less forgiving times.

Jerusalem Lane   89
   Represents a number of old roadways in and around the East
   Gwent area, that were once pilgrim trails, now signposted for
   tourists.

Bloodhouse   91
   Known as 'Ty Coch' literal translation 'Red House'.

About THE COLLECTIVE

The collective was formed in 1992 to provide an opportunity for poets and writers to publish their work.

Funding for each publication is raised through a series of poetry events held in Abergavenny (Y-Fenni), and the generosity of fellow writers and members of the public. No official of The Collective benefits from the funds raised.

If you are a writer or poet and would like to find out more about The Collective, please write to:

The Collective
Penlanlas Farm
Llantilio Pertholey
Y-Fenni
Gwent
NP7 7HN

With the support of
The Welsh Arts Council